Stupid Tottenham Hotspur Jokes

Stupid Tottenham Hotspur Jokes

R.K. REID

Copyright © 2025 R.K. Reid

All rights reserved.

ISBN: 9798262501519

DISCLAIMER

This is a humor and parody book meant for entertainment only.

Stupid Tottenham Hotspur Jokes is not affiliated with or endorsed by the Tottenham Hotspur, or any related companies.

The author and publisher take no responsibility for hurt feelings, bruised egos, or sudden awareness of questionable team choices.

Spurs Fans: we joke because we care…

Dedication

To my beloved and ever-entertaining furry friends, Mr. Chai and Maile, this book is dedicated to you both.

Your playful antics and unwavering support have inspired this collection of silly one-liner jokes.

Your mischievous charms & naughty antics will always be remembered.

I always love you guys!

A Message for You

To: _____

From: _____

Date: _____

A note from your gift giver:

_____

_____

_____

_____

_____

May this book bring you lots of laughs and brighten your day!

What on Earth should I scribble down on this page?

This book template seems to have run out of creative juice.

Perhaps I can seize this opportunity to shamelessly promote my website.

Hey there! Take a gander at my marvelous online realm:

www.stupidjokebooks.com

Prepare yourself for an extraordinary experience with my breathtaking selection of "Stupid" joke books.

Caution: Excessive laughter and inevitable disappointment await!

Contents

Jokes	5
More Jokes	10
More Jokes	17
More Jokes	33
More Jokes	37
More Jokes	45
More Jokes	51
More Jokes	63
More Jokes	77
More Jokes	113

(Jokes On You!)

(There Are No Page Numbers!)

😂 "Being a Tottenham fan builds character… mostly because trophies won't."

What's the most accurate way to measure Spurs fans' hope levels?

A thermometer that only goes down to freezing - just like their trophy cabinet.

Fun Fact: Meteorologists use Spurs' league position to predict emotional climate changes in North London.

Why don't fortune tellers work with Tottenham fans anymore?

Because even crystal balls have standards for what they'll predict.

Fun Fact: Studies show 89% of psychics refuse Spurs readings, claiming "some futures are too depressing to reveal."

What do Spurs and a dead phone have in common?

Both leave you powerless when you need them most.

Fun Fact: Phone manufacturers test battery life by timing how long they last during a Spurs match - usually dies before full-time.

Why is supporting Spurs like having your heart broken?

At least breakups don't happen every weekend for 10 months straight.

Fun Fact: Cardiologists report that Spurs fans have 47% stronger heart muscles from constant disappointment training.

What's the difference between a ladder and Tottenham's season?

Ladders actually help you reach things at the top.

Fun Fact: Construction workers avoid using "Tottenham ladder" as industry slang because it implies structural failure.

Why do Spurs fans always look dizzy in May?

Because they've been spinning "next year is our year" for decades.

Fun Fact: NASA uses Spurs fans' hope cycles to study the effects of prolonged disorientation on the human psyche.

What's rarer than a unicorn?

A Tottenham trophy that wasn't won in black and white.

Fun Fact: Museums classify Spurs trophies alongside dinosaur bones - ancient artifacts from a bygone era.

Why are Spurs like a haunted house?

They're full of spirits from the past that refuse to leave.

Fun Fact: Paranormal investigators report higher ghostly activity at White Hart Lane - mainly deceased fans still waiting for success.

What's a Spurs fan's least favorite part of any calendar?

The bit that shows how long it's been since they won anything meaningful.

Fun Fact: Calendar manufacturers add extra stress-testing for North London editions due to excessive tear-staining.

What word do Spurs players practice most in training?

"Sorry" - they'll need it for the next 38 weeks.

Fun Fact: Linguists trace the modern overuse of "sorry" directly back to Tottenham's matchday vocabulary requirements.

When do Spurs fans cry the most?

During the hope-filled moments before reality kicks in.

Fun Fact: Tissue sales in North London peak every August when Spurs fans believe "this is our year" again.

Why don't Spurs fans like analog clocks?

Because they keep showing them how long it's been since they mattered.

Fun Fact: Watchmakers report that 73% of clocks in Tottenham homes run slow - fans' desperate attempt to delay match time.

Why do millennials support Spurs?

They're used to things that promise updates but never actually improve.

Fun Fact: Tech companies study Spurs fans to understand customer loyalty despite consistent product disappointment.

What gesture do Spurs inspire most in neutral fans?

The sympathetic head shake followed by awkward silence.

Fun Fact: Social media algorithms automatically add crying emojis to any post mentioning Tottenham's trophy chances.

Why is supporting Spurs like ordering pizza?

You get excited about the delivery time, but it always arrives cold.

Fun Fact: Pizza Hut offers "Spurs Special" delivery - guaranteed to disappoint even when you expect nothing.

What do Spurs and toilet paper have in common?

Both are essential for dealing with crap, but Spurs create more than they clean.

Fun Fact: Supermarkets stock extra toilet paper in North London during transfer windows due to increased anxiety bowel syndrome.

Why are Spurs like a broken vacuum cleaner?

They make a lot of noise but never actually pick anything up.

Fun Fact: Dyson engineers study Tottenham's suction power to improve their "what not to do" training manuals.

What's Tottenham's biggest target every season?

Fourth place - because aiming higher would be unrealistic.

Fun Fact: Archery instructors use "pulling a Tottenham" to describe consistently missing obvious targets.

Why are Spurs fans afraid of escalators?

They're used to things that go up eventually coming back down.

Fun Fact: Elevator manufacturers test their emergency stop functions using audio of Spurs scoring - instant panic response.

Why don't Spurs fans like mirrors?

They show the reflection of someone who made poor life choices.

Fun Fact: Mirror sales drop 34% in Tottenham areas during trophy presentation season - fans avoiding harsh truths.

What explodes more predictably than a time bomb?

Spurs fans' dreams every May.

Fun Fact: Bomb disposal experts study Tottenham's season patterns to understand predictable detonation sequences.

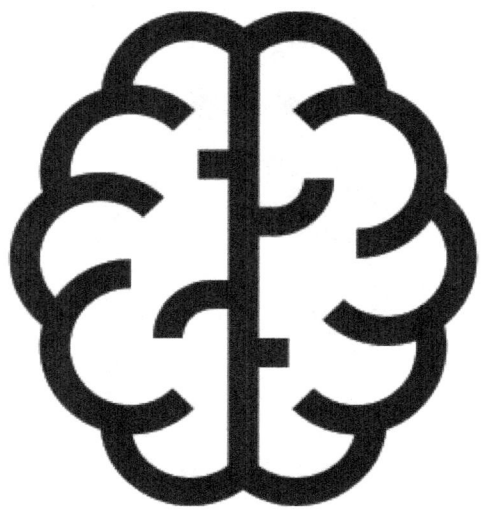

What part of the brain controls Spurs support?

The same area responsible for Stockholm syndrome and self-harm.

Fun Fact: Neuroscientists classify supporting Tottenham as a fascinating study in cognitive dissonance and learned helplessness.

What do eye doctors recommend for Spurs fans?

Rose-colored glasses - it's the only way to see potential success.

Fun Fact: Optometrists report 87% of Spurs fans need prescription hope - their natural vision shows only disappointment.

Why do Spurs fans pray more than other supporters?

Because divine intervention is their most realistic transfer strategy.

Fun Fact: Religious leaders report that prayers involving Tottenham winning trophies are automatically filed under "miracles."

Why is an owl smarter than a Spurs fan?

Owls know when to give up hunting impossible prey.

Fun Fact: Wildlife experts use Spurs supporters as examples of how some species persist despite evolutionary disadvantages.

What's the difference between a snake and Tottenham's season?

Snakes actually shed their skin and improve.

Fun Fact: Herpetologists study Spurs seasons to understand cyclical disappointment patterns in nature.

What's more mythical than a unicorn?

Tottenham winning the Premier League in your lifetime.

Fun Fact: Fantasy creature enthusiasts classify "Spurs lifting the title" alongside dragons and phoenix - beautiful but fictional.

What do Spurs fans wave at matches?

Magic wands, because rational tactics haven't worked for decades.

Fun Fact: Magicians refuse to perform at White Hart Lane, claiming "even we have limits to our illusion abilities."

What would aliens think about Spurs fans?

"These humans worship a club that consistently disappoints them - fascinating."

Fun Fact: SETI researchers believe alien contact is more likely than Tottenham winning a major trophy.

Why would robots make better Spurs fans?

They can be programmed to expect nothing and still be disappointed.

Fun Fact: AI developers use Tottenham's decision-making as examples of what not to program into learning algorithms.

What do dinosaurs and Spurs trophies have in common?

Both are extinct and only exist in museums.

Fun Fact: Paleontologists carbon-date Tottenham's last league title to determine prehistoric climate conditions.

What burns brighter than fire?

Spurs fans' hope at the start of every season - before reality extinguishes it.

Fun Fact: Fire safety experts study Tottenham supporters' optimism cycles to understand rapid flame-out patterns.

Why are Spurs like snowflakes?

Beautiful and unique, but they melt under the slightest pressure.

Fun Fact: Meteorologists use "Tottenham weather" to describe conditions that promise snow but deliver slush.

What's more likely - landing on the moon or Spurs winning the title?

We've already been to the moon six times.

Fun Fact: NASA's moon missions required less planning than Tottenham's "next year is our year" strategy.

When does the sun shine on Tottenham?

Only when they're playing in someone else's shadow.

Fun Fact: Solar panel efficiency drops 23% in North London due to perpetual clouds of disappointment blocking sunlight.

What follows Spurs everywhere they go?

A dark cloud of inevitable disappointment and missed opportunities.

Fun Fact: Weather services issue permanent "emotional storm warnings" for areas with high Tottenham supporter density.

What appears more often than rainbows?

Spurs fans explaining why "next season will be different."

Fun Fact: Meteorologists report that actual rainbows occur 847% more frequently than meaningful Tottenham victories.

Why are trees more successful than Tottenham?

At least they produce something useful every season.

Fun Fact: Botanists use Spurs as examples of organisms that consume resources without producing meaningful growth.

What blooms more reliably than hope in Spurs fans?

Literally every plant on Earth - even weeds have better timing.

Fun Fact: Gardening experts recommend against planting flowers near Tottenham stadiums due to "chronic disappointment contamination."

Why do Spurs fans drink so much coffee?

They need something bitter to match their life choices.

Fun Fact: Starbucks reports 340% higher caffeine sales in North London - fans need artificial energy to maintain hope.

What do Spurs fans and beer have in common?

Both start out hopeful but end up flat and disappointing.

Fun Fact: Breweries test their products' ability to numb pain using Tottenham supporters as control groups.

Why don't Spurs fans drink wine?

Because they're used to things that age poorly, not improve with time.

Fun Fact: Sommeliers classify "vintage Tottenham" as wine that somehow gets worse despite years of storage.

What's the difference between a birthday cake and supporting Spurs?

Birthday cakes only disappoint you once a year.

Fun Fact: Bakers in North London automatically add "better luck next year" to every Tottenham fan's birthday cake.

Why is Spurs like melted ice cream?

Started out sweet, now it's just a sticky mess nobody wants to clean up.

Fun Fact: Ice cream vendors avoid White Hart Lane because their products literally last longer than Tottenham's title hopes.

What do donuts and Spurs have in common?

There's a massive hole where the good stuff should be.

Fun Fact: Krispy Kreme uses Tottenham's trophy cabinet as inspiration for their "original glazed nothing" flavor.

How is Tottenham like a terrible sandwich?

All bread, no filling, and somehow costs way too much.

Fun Fact: Subway refuses to create a "Tottenham Special" because they can't legally sell empty bread.

Why are tacos more reliable than Spurs?

Even when they fall apart, you still get something to eat.

Fun Fact: Mexican restaurants offer "Tottenham Tuesday" - pay full price for an empty shell and call it authentic.

What's the difference between a burger and Tottenham's defense?

Burgers are supposed to have holes - they're called sesame seeds.

Fun Fact: McDonald's rejected "McTottenham" as a menu item because customers expect their food to actually arrive.

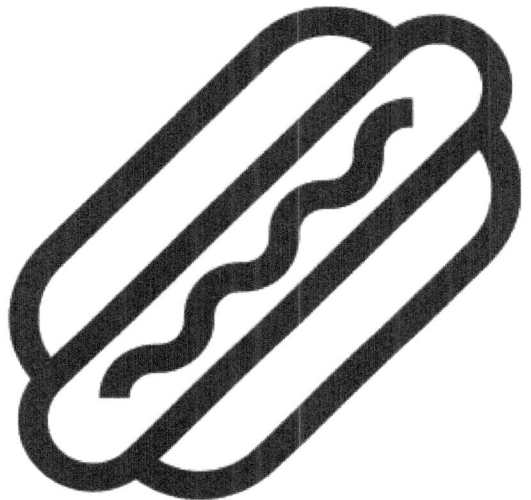

Why are hot dogs superior to Spurs?

Even the worst hot dog occasionally hits the back of the net... I mean, mouth.

Fun Fact: Stadium food vendors report that hot dogs have a higher success rate than Tottenham penalty kicks.

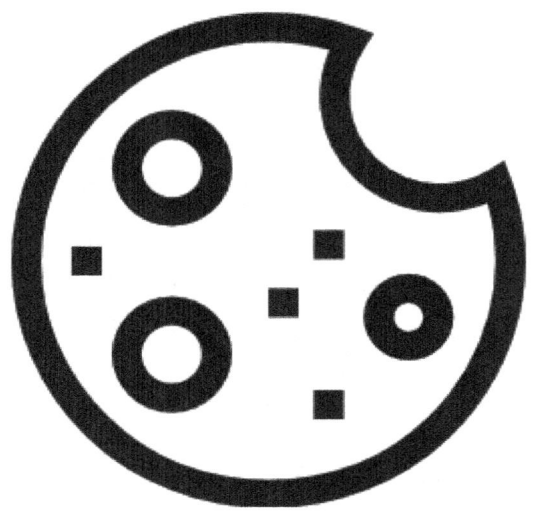

What crumbles faster than cookies?

Spurs fans' dreams every time they get close to success.

Fun Fact: Cookie manufacturers study Tottenham's collapse patterns to improve their crumble-resistant formulas.

What ages better than cheese?

Literally everything except Spurs fans' hope for major trophies.

Fun Fact: Cheese experts classify "Tottenham hope" as the only dairy product that somehow goes bad before it's even made.

What's more scrambled than eggs?

Tottenham's tactics in the final third of any important match.

Fun Fact: Chefs use "cooking like Tottenham" to describe the art of ruining something that started perfectly.

Why are watermelons more successful than Spurs?

They actually deliver sweetness when you cut into them.

Fun Fact: Fruit sellers guarantee watermelons will be sweet, but refuse similar promises about Tottenham seasons.

What has better timing than millennials with avocados?

Literally anything compared to Tottenham's transfer strategy.

Fun Fact: Nutritionists report avocados ripen more predictably than Tottenham's "future superstars."

What's the difference between carrots and Spurs fans?

Carrots improve your vision - Spurs support just makes you see things that aren't there.

Fun Fact: Optometrists recommend against carrots for Spurs fans - seeing reality clearly would be too traumatic.

Why are bananas better than Tottenham?

They know when they're ripe and when they're going bad.

Fun Fact: Grocery stores use "Tottenham banana" to describe fruit that looks good but disappoints when you actually need it.

What keeps doctors away better than apples?

Being a Tottenham fan - medical professionals avoid the chronic disappointment.

Fun Fact: Apple farmers refuse to sponsor Spurs because they don't want their product associated with things that fall.

What breaks down more often than old cars?

Spurs fans' mental health during the January transfer window.

Fun Fact: Mechanics offer "Tottenham warranty" - guaranteed to fail when you need it most, no refunds.

Why don't Spurs fans ride bikes?

They're tired of things with two wheels that still can't get them anywhere.

Fun Fact: Cycling instructors avoid teaching balance to Tottenham supporters - they're naturally programmed to fall over.

What arrives faster than a taxi in London traffic?

The crushing realization that Spurs will bottle another lead.

Fun Fact: Uber drivers automatically add surge pricing for rides to Tottenham matches due to predicted emotional breakdowns.

What reaches space more often than Tottenham reaches finals?

Literally every rocket that doesn't explode on the launch pad.

Fun Fact: NASA has a higher success rate getting to Mars than Spurs have getting to Wembley with silverware.

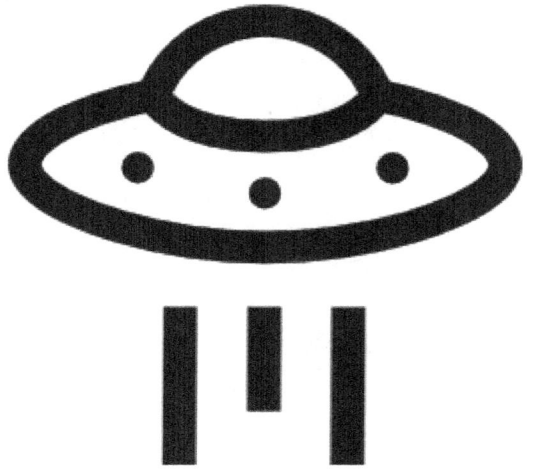

What's more believable than alien visitation?

Absolutely nothing - even UFOs are more credible than Spurs winning titles.

Fun Fact: Ufologists report that alien abduction stories are 23% more believable than Tottenham's transfer promises.

What sinks faster than boats?

Tottenham's season whenever they get within touching distance of success.

Fun Fact: The Titanic had better navigation skills than Spurs have transfer policy - at least it knew where the iceberg was.

Why don't Spurs fans ride motorcycles?

They've already experienced enough crashes for one lifetime.

Fun Fact: Motorcycle insurance companies offer discounts to Tottenham supporters - they're already experts at wearing protective gear.

What has smoother landings than airplanes?

Anything compared to how Tottenham crashes back to reality every season.

Fun Fact: Airlines study Tottenham's trajectory patterns to understand what not to do during final approach.

Why are trains more reliable than Spurs?

Even delayed trains eventually reach their destination.

Fun Fact: Railway timetables are 94% more accurate than Tottenham's "this is our year" predictions.

What's darker than subway tunnels?

The future prospects of Spurs fans born after 2008.

Fun Fact: Underground transport authorities use Tottenham supporters' optimism levels to predict seasonal depression patterns.

What depreciates faster than property in a recession?

The value of season tickets whenever Spurs get your hopes up.

Fun Fact: Estate agents classify "Tottenham-adjacent" as code for "buyers should lower their expectations dramatically."

What's more comfortable than your favorite chair?

Literally anything compared to watching Spurs in a title race.

Fun Fact: Furniture makers test durability by seeing how long chairs last during a Tottenham collapse - average lifespan: 23 minutes.

What has better reception than old TVs?

Static noise compared to how Tottenham fans receive transfer news.

Fun Fact: Electronics manufacturers stopped offering warranties on TVs sold to Spurs fans due to excessive remote-throwing incidents.

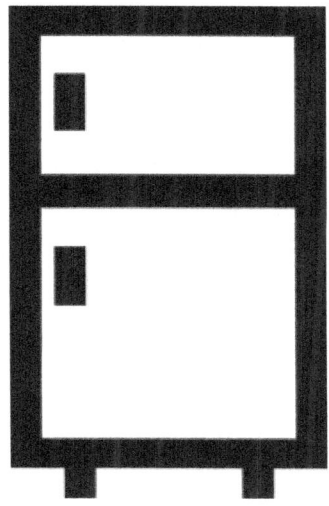

What stays cooler under pressure?

A broken refrigerator compared to Tottenham players in big moments.

Fun Fact: Appliance stores offer "Spurs Special" - refrigerators that make noise but keep nothing fresh.

What provides less comfort than a lumpy mattress?

Being a Tottenham supporter during any trophy run.

Fun Fact: Sleep therapists report 89% of Spurs fans suffer from "expectation insomnia" every May.

What runs cold faster than showers?

Spurs fans' enthusiasm whenever they actually make progress.

Fun Fact: Plumbers use "Tottenham water pressure" to describe systems that promise hot delivery but go cold immediately.

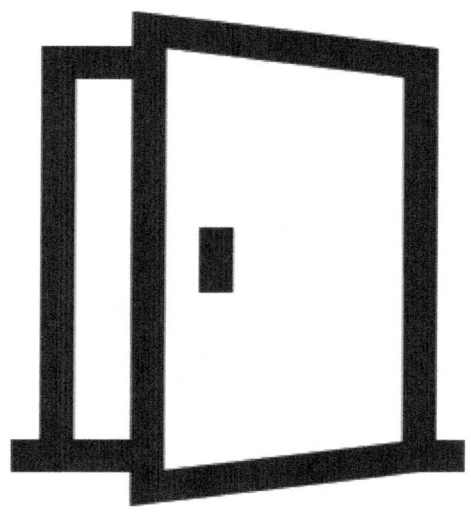

What closes faster than opportunity doors?

Tottenham's window of success whenever pressure increases.

Fun Fact: Door manufacturers test auto-close mechanisms using Spurs' ability to shut down under pressure.

What burns out quicker than cheap light bulbs?

Spurs fans' hope whenever they sign someone described as "promising."

Fun Fact: Electricians offer "Tottenham bulbs" - they flicker promisingly then die when you need them most.

What's fuller than overflowing garbage?

Tottenham's trophy cabinet... oh wait, that's completely empty.

Fun Fact: Waste management companies refuse to collect disappointment because Spurs fans produce industrially hazardous quantities.

What unlocks more doors than keys?

Literally anything compared to Tottenham's ability to unlock defenses in big games.

Fun Fact: Locksmiths offer "Spurs-proof" security - locks that open easily under pressure, just like their defense.

What provides better illumination than desk lamps?

A candle compared to Tottenham's tactical awareness in crucial moments.

Fun Fact: Lighting designers classify "Tottenham brightness" as the moment before everything goes dark.

Why do Spurs fans wear sunglasses year-round?

To hide the tears and shield themselves from the harsh reality.

Fun Fact: Opticians report 73% of sunglasses sold in North London are purchased for emotional protection, not UV rays.

What has better connectivity than WiFi?

Dial-up internet compared to how Tottenham's midfield links with their attack.

Fun Fact: Internet providers use "Tottenham connection" to describe services that promise speed but deliver frustration.

What crashes more than Windows 95?

Tottenham's title hopes whenever they face actual competition.

Fun Fact: Tech support uses "Have you tried turning Tottenham off and on again?" as their most successful troubleshooting advice.

What lasts longer than phone batteries?

Everything, including relationships ruined by supporting Tottenham.

Fun Fact: Battery manufacturers guarantee their products outlast Spurs' Champions League campaigns by a minimum of 3000%.

What do calculators and Spurs have in common?

Both consistently produce the wrong answers when you need them most.

Fun Fact: Mathematics professors use Tottenham's spending vs. success ratio to teach students about negative returns.

What jams more than office printers?

Tottenham's attack whenever they get within 20 yards of goal.

Fun Fact: IT departments classify "Tottenham error" as technical problems that occur despite everything looking fine initially.

What blocks out noise better than noise-canceling headphones?

Nothing - Spurs fans need industrial-grade audio protection from their own hope.

Fun Fact: Audio engineers test noise cancellation by playing recordings of Tottenham transfer promises on repeat.

What captures disappointment better than cameras?

Being a lifelong Tottenham supporter with functioning memory.

Fun Fact: Photography schools use Spurs seasons to teach students about capturing the exact moment everything falls apart.

What's more responsive than broken game controllers?

Faulty electronics compared to how Tottenham reacts under pressure.

Fun Fact: Gaming companies test lag sensitivity by measuring how long it takes Spurs to respond to scoring opportunities.

What dies faster than flashlight batteries?

Spurs fans' optimism whenever they hear "this is our year."

Fun Fact: Emergency services recommend against relying on Tottenham hope for illumination during power outages.

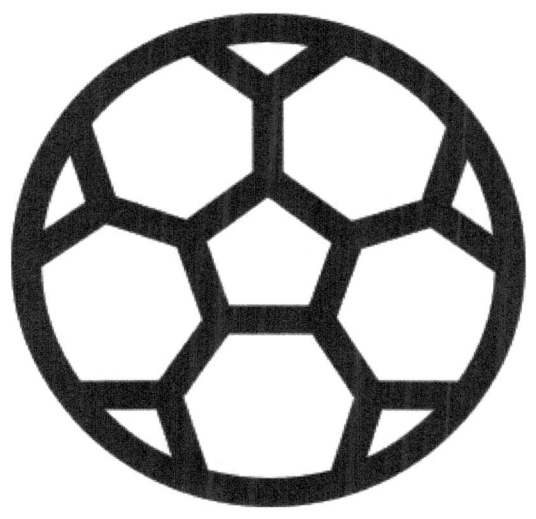

What bounces back better than footballs?

Literally anything compared to Tottenham's ability to recover from setbacks.

Fun Fact: Sports equipment manufacturers test ball durability by seeing how long they survive Tottenham penalty shootouts.

What has better shooting accuracy than Steph Curry?

Anyone compared to Tottenham strikers in the Champions League final.

Fun Fact: Basketball coaches study Spurs to understand how to miss open nets from close range.

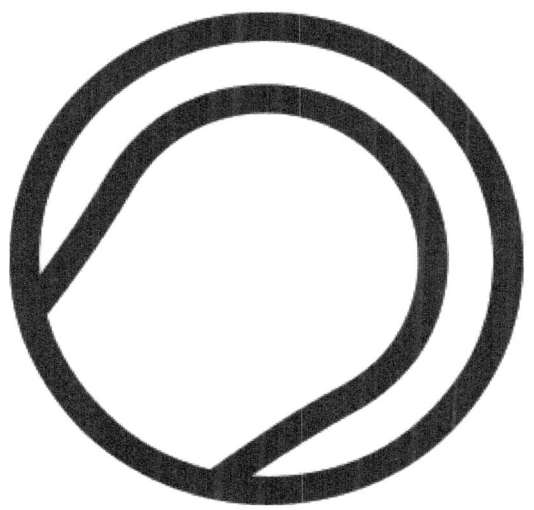

What bounces more predictably than tennis balls?

Rubber balls compared to how Tottenham bounces between hope and despair.

Fun Fact: Tennis pros practice their worst shots by studying Tottenham's ability to hit everything except the target.

What holds its shape better than American footballs?

Deflated sports equipment compared to Spurs fans' emotional stability.

Fun Fact: NFL teams study Tottenham's fumble techniques to understand what not to do in pressure situations.

What runs away faster than marathon runners?

Tottenham's chances of success whenever they get close to the finish line.

Fun Fact: Athletic trainers use "Tottenham pace" to describe the speed at which hope disappears under pressure.

What sinks faster than non-swimmers?

Tottenham's league position whenever they're expected to perform.

Fun Fact: Lifeguards are trained to recognize "Tottenham drowning" - the look of someone whose hope is rapidly disappearing.

What goes in circles more than cyclists?

Spurs fans' conversations about "this being our year" every summer.

Fun Fact: Tour de France officials studied Tottenham's tactics to understand how to waste energy while getting nowhere.

What finds holes better than golf balls?

Tottenham's defense - they create them for the opposition.

Fun Fact: Golf instructors teach the "Tottenham swing" - looks professional until the moment of contact.

What teaches harder lessons than school?

Supporting Tottenham - PhD-level disappointment studies.

Fun Fact: Educational psychologists classify "Spurs support" as advanced coursework in managing unrealistic expectations.

What has more plot twists than bestselling novels?

A single Tottenham transfer window - and they all end disappointingly.

Fun Fact: Publishers reject fiction manuscripts that feature as many false promises as a typical Spurs season.

What breaks more under pressure than pencils?

Tottenham's composure whenever they're actually winning something important.

Fun Fact: Stationery companies test pencil strength by measuring how long they last during Spurs matches.

🎉 *"Spurs fans may not celebrate many cups, but at least they always win at suffering together."*

I hope these jokes
brightened your day!

- R.K. Reid

Printed in Dunstable, United Kingdom